Dr Gayle Smerdon is a sociologist, consultant and author, whose work explores how we navigate the complex intersection of life, work and wellbeing. She helps people and organisations pause, consider and reshape how they live, lead and learn, turning chaos into clarity and intention into action.

Gayle's writing blends warmth, wit and evidence-based insights to make big ideas feel doable.

She lives in Melbourne and divides her time between writing, speaking and helping others make sense of their busy, beautiful lives. When she's not at her desk chasing ideas or deep in research, Gayle is happily serving her feline overlord, Mr Spooks.

Also by Gayle Smerdon PhD

Do ONE THING and Do It Deep:
How to focus and energise your workplace

iDevelop:
How to take charge of your professional development by becoming a conscious learner

THE BAD DAY PLAYBOOK

What to do when everything sucks

Dr Gayle Smerdon

BROADCAST

To everyone who has ever helped create a Bad Day,
thank you for the research material.

To everyone who's helped me through one, thank you
for the rescue missions, large and small.

And to everyone still figuring it out, may you meet
yourself with kindness, even on the messy days.

Contents

Dear Bad Day, we need to talk	**7**
Abandon despair, all ye who enter here	**20**
Part 1 – I just don't know what to do with myself	**24**
Check the basics	**26**
Understand the variables	**31**
Don't fuel the Bad Day fire	**34**
Make your choice	**37**
Part 2 – What's your play?	**52**
The Bad Day Playbook Model	**55**
Reflect	**56**
Talk	**76**
Distract	**98**
Play	**118**
What if it doesn't work?	**138**
Part 3 – Let's not go there	**148**
Good, bad or something else	**151**
Being a bit stoic	**154**
A proactive playbook	**156**
Contacts	**160**
Bad Day resources	**164**
Endnotes	**165**

The best way to not feel hopeless is to get up and do something. Don't wait for good things to happen to you. If you go out and make some good things happen, you will fill the world with hope, you will fill yourself with hope.[1]

Barack Obama

Dear Bad Day, we need to talk

If you have picked up this book and are in the middle of a Bad Day, you want answers and not a whole lot of beautiful, if quirky, writing. (Sad face in words.)

Take a breath. I'm here to help.
Here is what you need right here, right now.

At its heart, this book aims to help you find ONE THING you can do to manage your Bad Day better.

Let me boil it down for you.

If you are experiencing a Bad Day, you need to answer three questions. Your answers will direct you to a specific chapter where you can choose from a menu of things to do right this minute. Something to help break the spell of the Bad Day Genie. Because nothing beats a Bad Day like taking back control – whatever that looks like for you right now.

Ready? Then answer these questions.

1

Do you want to do something about your Bad Day?

If the answer is **No**, that's fine.

Go straight to the chapter 'Make your choice' and find the section called 'Staying stuck', so you can get on with your Bad Day-ness.

If the answer is **Yes**, go to the next question.

2

Do you want to be by yourself with your Bad Day-ness (Going Alone), or do you need some company (Going Together)?

Choose either **Going Alone** or **Going Together** and move on to the final question.

3

Do you want to reflect on what's causing your current Bad Day-ness (Going In), so you can get to the nub of it? Or do you want to distract yourself (Going Out)?

Choose either **Going In** or **Going Out**.

Okay, well done. You are taking control.

THE BAD DAY PLAYBOOK MODEL

The field of play

Now, let's check out The Bad Day Playbook Model. Think of it like a playing field. Once you know your position, you'll know your best next move.

If you decided not to do anything about your Bad Day, then you are already reading 'Staying stuck'.

Otherwise, it's time for you to locate your answers to Questions 2 and 3 in the model.

It's pretty straightforward, but let's take an example. If you decide you need to be by yourself and don't really want to deal with too much right now, you will have chosen Go It Alone and Go Out. That puts you in the Distract quadrant of the model.

Hurry! Start finding things to do straight away to take charge of your Bad Day-ness.

Go straight to Part 2, 'What's your play', and find the chapter called 'Distract'.

You will find out what Distract is all about – what's good about embracing this approach, and what some of the pitfalls may be.

Select ONE THING from the activities on offer. And then do that.

Why?

Because nothing is going to help more than taking deliberate action.

And while skipping off straightaway to take action – good on you! – will help you immediately, you will miss some of the critical nuances, caveats and amusing and insightful stories in the rest of the book. I hope you will come back to the beginning later.

Now, if you are still reading this section and haven't zoomed off to find instant relief, there's a few other things to know about The Bad Day Playbook Model.

It is not a deeply scientific study. It's mainly a super-helpful model to point you towards choosing and taking action that will assist in changing your state of mind when you are stuck. But there is some good research that grounds our understanding of why things might or might not be beneficial.

Another thing you should know is that, generally, I don't like telling people what they should be doing (although some family members might disagree). I like setting out some strategies, sharing a few useful tools, and coaching people to think about what *they* want to do. So I'm more about the 'How' than the 'What'.

I'm not trying to solve whatever problem you have. I'm just giving you some pointers on how you can get out of the stuck-ness at critical times. It's not an individual step-by-step solution. Think of it more like a signpost pointing the way to the travel section in a bookstore, directions to where you can browse all the places you could choose to go and find out a bit about them before you do. Everyone will take their own journey, in their own way, at their own pace.

I don't know what brought you to Bad Day Island, but this book can help you reach a place where you can start to deal with it, move past it, or work through it.

The first part of this playbook shows you around the field of play. It explains some preliminary things about managing your Bad Day and helps you get clear on your Bad Day category.

Part Two focuses on the different things you can do to 'un-suck' your day and get you through it, now that you've decided on the kind of action you need. Because your Bad Day brain is impinging on your ability to think clearly, this section is a handy reference, full of possibilities to choose from.

Once you are through the worst, the final part gives you a different way to think about Bad Day-ness in the future and how to limit its impact. What is your preventative Bad Day care plan? How will you notice when you are on the path to Bad Day-ness?

And, for the record, there are at least two good reasons for making the time to think about doing more than addressing the current Bad Day experience. One reason is you, and the other is everyone else around you. And that's because ongoing Bad Days are a concern for your mental and physical health, as well as being highly contagious and potentially harmful to others.

Caveat

Let's be clear. This is a book for addressing everyday troubles. It's both serious in its endeavour to provide a handy guide to help you out of a bit of a funk, and just a little flippant.

It doesn't offer medical or psychological advice and isn't suitable for those suffering from any form of serious mental illness. It won't address a deep existential crisis – and what's the likelihood of humankind experiencing that anytime soon?

I hope this book and its suggestions help you. Having created a list of things to try to refocus myself has helped me. However, if your Bad Day gets stuck in a repeat cycle or becomes particularly bad, don't put off seeking professional assistance. Reach out to your doctor, call Lifeline or contact one of the suggested organisations listed at the back of the book.

I'm just going to put an 'out of order' sticker on my forehead and call it a day.[2]

Abandon despair, all ye who enter here

As a baby ... toddler ... child ... teenager ... okay, all my life, I have been an expert in expressing to all those around me when I was having a Bad Day. Being a generous soul, I could share all manner of Bad Day-nesses with others.

As a kid, my pouty bottom lip was a telltale sign of impending Bad-icity. Then, as I grew older, I developed many more ways of demonstrating my frustration and anger at a world failing to meet my expectations. And somewhere along the way, I also became much better at internalising. I often felt that, somehow, I was more at fault than the world – and sometimes that was true. My brittle confidence was easily and frequently damaged or broken. I managed to hide this with bravado for a while, but eventually that collapsed as well.

Bad Days waxed, but more often waned, as I grew older. But they are always there. Waiting. Ready to pounce. Like a shadow poised for the sun to be at just the right angle.

I recall one afternoon, a little while ago now, I found myself in the Bad Day Position – sitting slumped on the couch, unable to move any part of my body because someone had turned gravity up, throat closing over and tears pending. On this occasion, it was merely an extended series of unfortunate events and exhaustion that had taken me there. I had not noticed the slow accumulation of negative thoughts, and I had been ignoring my physical and emotional needs. All of which finally led to the last straw breaking the camel's back.

After some time sitting with my despair, I wondered what would make me feel better.

I had no idea.

When you are in full-on Bad Day mode, you don't always have a ready path for getting out of it. Your ability to think, plan or create options has been decimated by the body's chemical reaction to stress, as it overloads you with hormones to help you run away or punch someone.

While I had no idea what the answer was, I had a question. What would help? And a question gives me something to solve.

I decided that what I really needed in that situation was a list or a guide. Something that could help me when my brain, heart and body could not move me to a more positive state. I needed to see a few options – things I could attempt to start shifting the Bad Day-ness dial. They needed to be outside of my head because, in this state, inside my head was a complete mess and very unreliable. So perhaps having something written down on a page would help.

I began to make a list on my phone. Now, the ideas were there, but they were all over the place, which became frustrating. The list wasn't specific enough, or put together in a way that would help me decide what action to take. But then, one morning as I was showering, I had an idea (all my ideas happen in the shower) for a model that could at least help narrow things down. I found it quite a useful way to think about my Bad Days.

And so, gentle readers, after some research and chatting with lots of people, here we are. Hopefully, with a playbook for those times when you or someone you love is having a Bad Day. Something to help you take that one tiny step that can move you to less-Bad.

Welcome to *The Bad Day Playbook*.

Part 1
I just don't know what to do with myself

Except for a couple of perfect and annoying people you know, everybody, everywhere, will experience the odd Bad Day sometimes.

And two things.

First, you are wrong about those 'perfect' people.

Second, how lucky are we if it's just the odd day?

Before we get into this any further, I have a couple of really obvious things you need to ask yourself if you are experiencing a Bad Day.

Check the basics

Have you eaten?

Yes, folks, sometimes it's that simple. Maybe your blood sugar has dropped or you are dehydrated. It's hard to think clearly when that happens. So ask yourself when you last had something to drink or if you need a snack. Get some food and liquid into you.

Now, I've noticed that while hydration is generally a given, there are two opposing types of popular advice when it comes to what to eat if you are having a Bad Day.

The first suggests the importance of eating healthy foods that help regulate your brain and body to aid a faster recovery. You can search the internet for these types of food recommendations, but the advice can be a little inconsistent. Somehow the top seven foods are never the same seven foods.

Try experimenting with some of the suggested foods you already like. The day is bad enough already without forcing down foods that make you want to barf.

The second theme is oriented towards comfort foods. These are usually very individual and relate to memories of family favourites and treats from your childhood. Sometimes, these preferences are part of a larger cultural story. Either way, my research reveals that cheese seems to feature, especially grilled cheese sandwiches, mac and cheese, and pizza. And potato – mashed or fries. And chocolate. And ice-cream. Actually, now that I look at it, there are quite a few ways to go here.

I am not going to judge you. I am also not a dietitian. Personally, I try to avoid fast-metabolising, sugary foods and drinks. My go-to foods are nuts and cheese. The exception is when I start feeling shaky. Then I incorporate a sugary snack as well. But there are also times when I find myself out of control, trying to fill that black hole of emotional need with handy treats. So, as I say, no judgement.

Falling back on emotional eating is a natural human response. We connect eating with early memories of care and being nurtured. Plus, chewing has a soothing effect on us. However, if this response becomes a habit then that can be a problem, and you might want to get some information and help with that.[3]

Was it a bad day?
Or was it a bad five minutes
that you milked all day?[4]

Do you need a nap?

The other common issue is that sometimes we are tired. Many people are exhausted due to their work, other life responsibilities, and the expectations of what it means to be good and successful in our culture.

The fix for this isn't always straightforward, and whether you can respond right away will depend on your situation. If you are in the middle of a meeting, it could be tricky. Those with small children or caring responsibilities may not be able to stop everything to take a nap or even simply relax. I know that some parents cannot go to the bathroom without the insistent company of their inexhaustible tiny humans, so that nap would be out of the question.

But otherwise, if you need to rest, and you can, then do it. Remember that you are a grown-up now. Stop walking around and saying you're tired; instead, take a break and recharge.

If you decide you can't rest, can you find a way? We sometimes default to 'No' when there might be some help we could call on, or a creative way for us to get even some of the rest we truly need. Find your sweet spot between being irresponsible by ignoring pressing responsibilities to get some shut-eye, and being a martyr and forging on relentlessly.

Our culture sends us messages that if we are not actively working, then we are lazy, and that makes us feel worthless. But resting is natural, healthy and our right. We can't think properly if we are tired. It's well established that sleep deprivation has a similar impact to being drunk.[5] Being human means getting the rest you need.

Now we have taken care of the obvious, let's step back and take in the view that is the grey looming shadow of an impending Bad Day.

Understand the variables

Thinking about what would help me on my most recent couch-bound, cranky-pants Bad Day, it seemed apparent that I only had two variables to play with – the intensity of the Bad and the length of time of the Bad.

Degrees of Bad

Bad comes in all shapes, sizes, flavours, textures and colours. Keep in mind that the degree of Bad-ness, or any pain, is relative. One person's Bad can be another person's okay and someone else's torture. But generally speaking, less Bad clearly seems better. Would we be quite as scared of the small bad wolf?

Limiting or at least not escalating the degree of Bad-ness is really the point of this book.

Length of time

It's handy to think of what's happening in terms of time. We say a 'Bad Day' out of habit. But no one said it had to be a whole day. Equally, no one said it had to be just one day. So, we can wrestle back a little control by thinking about timeframes.

One of the useful things this book does is shrink the length of our Bad Day time.

If you are having a Bad Day, how do you influence the time you are experiencing the Bad (nominally, a day) to be longer or shorter? And how do you effectively decrease the intensity of the Bad-ness?

Perhaps a good place to start is to not keep feeding the beast.

Don't fuel the Bad Day fire

There is a lot of pressure on people these days to get over a Bad Day quickly. To always be up and positive. It's like it is just not healthy or acceptable to be anything but super joyful every minute. Even at funerals we are expected to celebrate life, regardless of whether we are grieving or mourning. The resilience police might give you a second or two to bounce back, but after that, if you haven't found some useful way to rebound, learn from this experience and pivot to build your next empire out of it, you can start to feel less than competent. And comparing yourself with how well others appear to be doing is just going to hasten the downward spiral.

We all live and work in a 'self' that is not really optimal for the modern world. The 'self' was designed to survive in the savannah eons ago. It's not what you'd build for your modern 'self'. And when we try things out and they go wrong, many of us have a tendency to blame ourselves. Our chattering mind steps up to point out in no uncertain terms just how distant our reality is from our expectations. What a loser.

But if we can remember that we are working with a very old operating system, maybe we can be a bit forgiving when things go pear-shaped.

I like this advice from Peter Cook, which is that when things are not working well, we can do small life experiments. Try an adjustment where, for the next few months, you meditate each day or perhaps you stop work at a particular time – and see if it helps your 'self' to operate more optimally.

> The mistake is that when it doesn't work, we blame ourselves. We think, 'I'm weak', 'I'm not disciplined', or 'I'm wrong.' But it's much more useful to say, 'Oh! I didn't get the environment quite right', or 'I didn't get the structures quite right', or 'That wasn't the way to get the best out of me, so let me try something else.'[6]

Give yourself a break. Be kind, unwind.

Nothing is permanent in this world, not even our troubles.[7]

Charlie Chaplin

Make your choice

Everyone has Bad Days. It's what you do with them that matters. When you are spiralling into Bad Day-ness, you can choose to do one of several things, including staying stuck.

But if stuck-ness isn't your preferred option, at least for the long term, we are going to look at a couple of choices you can make to help navigate your way from Bad to not-so-Bad, good, or even great.

The first choice to make is whether you want to Go It Alone or if you need some company and prefer to Go Together.

GO IT ALONE　　　　　　　　　　　　　　**GO TOGETHER**

The second choice is whether you want to Go In and try to work this whole thing out. Or if you need to Go Out and give yourself a break from whatever is going on.

GOING IN　　　　　　　　　　　　　　　**GOING OUT**

Alone or Together? Going In or Going Out?

Answering these two questions will help you locate some activities to experiment with in your quest for a less long and/or less intense Bad Day.

No judgement. Each approach is appropriate at some point, and each has its downside. It's a good idea to consider both.

Let's look at those now.

Go It Alone

On some Bad Days, you can't or don't want to face other people. You just want to Go It Alone. Sometimes, you don't want to share your Bad-icity with your nearest and dearest. Maybe you decide that quarantine is the best option right now. You need some time and space.

 **Upside**

Whatever has happened, you've decided to do something about it yourself. It's by yourself and for yourself. You've got this. You're planning to take some action.

 **Downside**

When you're having a Bad Day, you may not be the best person for the job of getting you through it. You may be poorly equipped to assess and deal with the situation, given your current state. If you are stressed, anxious or sad, your brain is not in the best state to come up with creative ideas to move through this right now.

So, if you choose to Go It Alone, it's very, very, very important you keep monitoring yourself. Bad Days can be like quicksand and the ill-equipped can sink deeper. Consider whether you need an anchor post, so if you feel the ground softening further you can hold on and call for help. Let someone know your situation and that you want to spend some time reflecting.

Whoa! Really? That sounds awkward.

But it needn't be.

What I usually do is say, 'Hey, there. I'm just getting in touch to say Hi and that I'm having a bit of a crappy day. I don't want to get into it now, but can I get in touch later if I need to chat? I'll let you know either way. Thanks.'

Go Together

I can't emphasise enough how important it is to know that you don't need to do this alone. When you are not feeling up to handling a situation by yourself, being willing to seek support is a very grown-up thing to do. But it's important to consider who the right 'someone' is and how they can help. Will they bring the *energy*, *empathy* and *experience* you need?

I was just about to quit my postgraduate studies. My supervisor was never available, and when he was, he had a way of keeping me constantly changing directions. I didn't know what I was doing. I was confused, frustrated and felt very stupid. After trying to cope for quite a while, I thought it best if I just quit. I obviously wasn't cut out for this. But just before I did, I reached out to a lecturer from my previous university.

I told him what was happening and how I was feeling. He said, 'What are you doing hanging around with those dickheads? Let me help you find the right person to support you.'

Some days, you just need to connect with someone who believes in you when you can't.

 **Upside**

I love the saying, 'A problem shared is a problem halved.' You've identified that you might need some help with this. Good job.

Sometimes, people feel that if they can't handle their Bad Day sitution themselves, it means they are weak. Or they worry that no one would want to help them when they have ugly-cry-face and can't stammer coherently through sentences. But finding the right someone can bring a fresh perspective to what's happening. When we can't get the distance and perspective we need, or don't know what to do next, getting support is vital.

I can't remember where I saw this, but I recall a cartoon of two chickens standing across the road from each other. One chicken shouts, 'How do I get to the other side?' And the other chicken shouts back, 'You are on the other side.'

Just saying, a new perspective can really help.

 **Downside**

There is another, more cynical version of the saying I mentioned before. It says, 'A problem shared is now a problem two people have.' That's funny. But don't let my hilariousness influence your decision to go accompanied on this journey.

So, here are a few words of caution.

Are you looking to make someone else responsible for the problem and seeking a saviour? Keep in mind that you can't take the lifeguard home from the pool and that, at some point, you need to learn to swim.

Are you just looking for a chance to whinge? It's okay to blow off steam, but if you bring someone in to help you, plan on moving through or around your Bad Day with their support. Otherwise, you are just stuck and you've invited a friend along to be your audience.

If you seek someone to collaborate on your Bad Day, you will have many more. Don't look at someone else as your opportunity to avoid responsibility and hand over your power to them. That will come back to bite you.

Going In

So, you're Going In. You want to find a (deeper) resolution to your Bad Day. Choosing to go in means you are ready to be curious, do the work, get a better understanding of what the heck is going on, and see where that takes you. With a bit of digging, you may be able to shine a light on what this whole Bad Day is about and how not to have the same Groundhog Bad Day over and over and over again.

 **Upside**

Going In shouldn't sound all dark and mysterious. Staying curious about what's happening in your life is really healthy. And that's all of life – the good, the Bad and the beige. Rather than taking on the mantle of some deep therapeutic event, hold it a little more lightly and be genuinely curious as you seek to understand the mystery that is the human being called [*Your name here*].

But you've chosen to get to the bottom of this in order to get on top of it. Yes, our language is often strange. Even stranger, a quote on the www says, 'You can't get to the top by sitting on your bottom.'[8] It can feel a bit brave, but by deciding to try to get to the bottom of this early, you can stop yourself from hitting rock bottom. So, if getting to the bottom is important, be ready for a little Bad Day colonic irrigation and flush that sucker out. Okay, that metaphor has got way out of control.

 **Downside**

Choosing to go in can take you to unexpected places, so be prepared. It can be like picking a scab, and you know that is not what heals a wound. Fun fact, we don't leave wounds to dry out these days. We cover them in lovely little dressings that protect them from further external damage and germs, while helping the lymphocytes gather around the wound, keeping it moist and enabling the repair process.

If you need professional help, know where to find it. It isn't in this cute book. It's not with a friend. It's not working through something yourself. If there is a chance this *might* be you, there are some contact numbers at the back of the book. You don't need to reinvent the whole of psychology or counselling by yourself. Others have been working on some useful stuff for decades. Get in touch with them.

Going Out

Not dealing is perfectly acceptable – for now. On some Bad Days, it can feel like you just need to breathe for a moment. The best thing you can do is get out of your own way and escape for a while. Doing other things to take your mind off your Bad Day is an absolutely valid lifestyle choice. Have some fun and forget your cares and woes.

 Upside

There are days when you have to let it go and give yourself some space and look for some perspective. I remember one deeply Bad Day, getting home from work to find my housemate was having an equally Bad Day. We had very little money, rent due, and a giant black cloud hovering above our respective heads. We looked at each other and said, 'F@#* it, let's go out for dinner.'

We had a scrummy, expensive-ish dinner, wine and lush dessert, talked and laughed and came home feeling a lot better and ready to tackle things head-on. I'm not advocating this youthful irresponsibility as the salve for all woes. I'm just saying that I have never forgotten it. And now, recalling it is enough to remind me that life can be fun and tasty.

 **Downside**

There are many potential upsides to getting out and doing something to take your mind off your Bad Day. But (and this is a big but), if you never look at what's happening, at the situations, thoughts and behaviours that contributed to your Bad Day, you will be doomed to repeat them. And at some point, Sisyphus must have said to himself, 'I really hate this rock.'

Remember, distraction will only ever work for so long, but sometimes it's enough to break a Bad Day spell.

The first two choices are whether to go alone or accompanied, and then whether to go in or out. We are narrowing it down. But first, what if your choice is not to choose? What if you just stay stuck? And that is certainly an option.

If every day is a gift then today was socks.[9]

Staying stuck

You can choose to stay stuck in your own personal Bad Day black hole. Not to get overly technical, but here's how NASA describes black holes to Year 5–8 students.

> A black hole is a region in space where the pulling force of gravity is so strong that light is not able to escape. The strong gravity occurs because matter has been pressed into a tiny space. Because no light can escape, black holes are invisible.[10]

Yes, it can feel just like that. Overwhelmingly forceful. As if there is no escape.

You may think there are rational, understandable, unavoidable reasons for your current sense of stuck-ness, but you still need to decide what to do about it – even if it's nothing.

And the thing about stuck is that you often don't know you are there. You don't always see it coming. You are unaware and, therefore, you remain stuck.

So, the first and most important thing is to acknowledge it. See it as a black hole of Bad Day-ness, so at least you know what you are dealing with. Give it a name, if you like. Knowing that you are stuck means you have already started to shift.

It might not be true that when you are stuck, the only way is up, but at least there is usually a lot more up than down. When you know where you are, you can do something about it. But I have grave doubts about the up-and-down metaphor being helpful. It's possible the only way is through. As the saying goes, 'If you're going through hell, keep going.'[11]

 Upside

Staying stuck is great because it takes no effort. You can let yourself wallow, feel hard done by, whinge and complain, and generally not have to try. Plus, you are already exhausted, so staying here conserves your immediate energy, and you don't have to do anything about the soft hissing sound that is your mojo continuing to leak away.

 **Downside**

The downside of staying stuck is that you're stuck (d'oh!) and it can be hard to know you're there. Staying stuck escalates the length of time and the intensity of the Bad. The abyss that is your Bad Day can suck in more of yourself and affect those around you. It can send you on an increasing spiral of despair. One friend of mine described it as getting in a rut and moving the furniture in.

But if you are going to stay stuck, go at it. Really feel your stuck-ness, your frustrations, anger, whatever it is. Name it. Just be there in your stuck.

I often find that by giving my stuck 100 per cent all-in, everything I have, I get over it either through exhaustion or tedium, and want to move on to something else. Maybe give that a red-hot go.

It is your choice. However, might I suggest some other things you may like to try?

Now that you have chosen not to stay stuck, have answered the questions and located your choice in the model, it's time to toddle off and find the chapter that relates to that quadrant. There you'll find the upsides, potential downsides, and a list of things you might like to try to change your Bad to better.
It's time to make your play.

THE BAD DAY PLAYBOOK MODEL

The Bad Day Playbook Model

There are around 15 different activities listed under each of the four quadrants for you to choose from, as you dig into or distract yourself from your Bad Day experience. Browse your options and select something that you think could set you on the right path. Maybe it's familiar and comfortable, or maybe you want to give something new, a bit different and just outside your comfort zone a go. Make a choice and have a try!

If you haven't managed to be that decisive or want to keep your options open, read on as we look at each of the four quadrants – Reflect, Talk, Distract and Play.

You may want to adapt the activities to better suit your situation. Maybe a solo thing takes your fancy, but you want to bring a friend along. Group, two-player and solo activities can always be adjusted. So, reading – or flicking – through all the ideas could be helpful.

And you don't need to stop with the suggestions in this handsome little book. There is some space at the back of each section where you can write some of your own favourite ways to thoughtfully engage with your Bad Day-ness, either alone or in company, by giving yourself a break or getting into it. Then they are there ready if you need them in the future.

Reflect

You've decided to be alone for a while, just you and your Bad Day taking a long, hard look at each other. Good for you! (So that you know, I am going to say that every time.)

You are going to handle this by taking a deep breath and looking at what the heck is going on in your Bad Day-ness. You are going to sit with it for a while and then try to understand what it's telling you. Pick it up, turn it around, tip it upside-down and give it a bit of a shake.

 **Upside**

If you are confident in your ability to Go It Alone, then sit with whatever this is, move through it, and possibly begin to understand what's causing your Bad Day. You might start to notice patterns in your behaviour and thinking. By trying to find out what's going on, you can identify what could be effective in stopping this from happening again, or at least give you a bit of a heads-up and help you see it coming.

 **Downside**

If you are not feeling equipped to deal with Going In Alone, don't do it. Ask yourself if you have the physical, mental and emotional skills and energy – or can you find them relatively easily? You do not want to get stuck in the problem, or let your stress-affected brain come up with crappy ideas or solutions.

If this is your choice but you find it isn't going well, get help. If you sense you are falling into the trap of negatively ruminating, move to a Distract, Talk or Play option for a little while first. Have a plan in place and know who you can contact.

And just to remind you again, this book isn't a resource for those suffering a serious emotional crisis or mental illness. That's a whole other thing that needs professional help. There are resources listed at the back of the book that might be useful when you're looking for this kind of help. This book is for that Bad Day that is a bit sticky or repetitive.

Now if you are ready, it's time to dive in and see what you can do. I'll be waiting for you on the not-as-Bad side.

Nature bathing

Take a solitary walk and immerse yourself in the sights, sounds and scents of nature. Visit a forest, beach, river, botanical garden or park and get lost in the sensations of your environment – the rustling trees, the clouds floating by, the water flowing or waves washing to the shore.

Find ways to connect and ground yourself by walking barefoot on soft grass, digging your toes in the sand, or enjoying the feeling of dangling your feet in the water.

Explore. Breathe deeply. Feel a greater sense of tranquillity. Then, begin to reflect on your current situation by asking yourself some compassionate questions. For example, 'How healthy is my current perspective?', 'Will this matter in a few years' time?', 'What advice would your compassionate-self offer?'

Write it

Writing can calm the chaos, whether you're pouring your heart out or emptying your cranky bin. Grab a notebook, your favourite pen, and let your thoughts tumble out – doodles, rambles, mind maps, whatever wants to appear.

No editing, no judgement.

Or go the Bad Writing route and furiously record every annoying, frustrating, petty thing that's cluttering your head.

No filter. No finesse. Then rip it up into satisfyingly small pieces and bin it. Or safely burn it.

Two ways in, one goal: get it out of your head and onto the page.

Mindful moments

Find a comfy spot. Close your eyes. Then let your breath be your anchor. No need to 'do it right'. Just be here now.

Not sure how to start? Try a meditation app or simply notice your thoughts like clouds passing by. No judgement, just observation.

A wise mentor told me that this practice can be as simple as sitting down, closing your eyes and turning the corners of your mouth into a smile.

Don't get hung up on doing it right. Don't worry about failing. Keep breathing. Let go. Notice what shifts, even just a little.

Artistic expression

Grab whatever art supplies call to you – pencils, paint, paper, glue, or even Play-Doh. Let your hands do the talking.

Create without rules. Don't judge. Don't overthink. Just begin, even if you sit with a blank page for a while first.

Let whatever's inside come through. It doesn't need to be pretty. It just needs to be honest.

Art helps us release and reflect, and sometimes we surprise ourselves.

See what shows up that can enlighten you in the darkness of your Bad Day.

Immerse in music

Music can evoke emotions, enhance mood, and create a serene environment for introspection. Put on something gentle – instrumental, ambient, or anything that helps you slow down and breathe. Let it carry your thoughts, soften the edges of the day, and make space for calmness, emotions or insights to appear.

There is considerable research on the benefits of classical music on stress, anxiety and mood.[12] But if that's not your cup of tea, settle into something where you don't need to think too hard. Just listen. Let yourself rest and repair, as you gently and compassionately reflect on your situation.

Get moving

Aerobic exercise is a great way to lift your mood.[13] Use the rhythm of your steps during a solo run, jog or walk; the soft whirr as you peddle your bike; or the swoosh of your strokes as you swim to clear your mind and allow your thoughts to arise, and you have time to reflect.

I love getting into the pool. The water takes my weight and creates a feeling of support. I focus on the black line and count strokes to the end of the pool before tumble-turning and starting again.

But you do you.

Clearing your mind through physical activity sets you up for a clearer and better perspective on what's happening. It can even let it just slip away completely. No big deal.

Floral focus

Arrange a little joy by picking up some blooms. You can go foraging in your garden or grab some stems from the florist. They don't have to be fancy, just fresh and chosen with care.

Take your time arranging them. Breathe in the scent, feel the stillness, enjoy their magnificence, even if you are not a masterful floral arranger.

Place them somewhere you'll notice them often, as a quiet reminder that beauty doesn't need to shout.

I find this very centring on a Bad Day. The delicate blooms remind me of the fragility and beauty of this wacky world, helping me accept and release some of the crazy.

Explore the stars

Step outside on a clear night, look up and let the stars do their magical, mystical thing. Maybe settle in a little. Bring snacks, stretch out under the sky, and wrap up warmly if you need to.

There's no requirement to know the names of the constellations. Use an app if you're curious. You could let it be a mystery. Or do what I do and make up your own humorous names.

Let the vastness calm you. Allow the sense of awe to lighten your mind and your heart. Calibrate just how much the Bad Day really matters in the scheme of things, release what you can't control into the darkness and see the things you can do clearly.

Mindful gardening

There's something deeply therapeutic about getting your hands in the soil and tending to plants with care. Gardening slows you down and offers a quiet space to reflect on what you need to feel nourished, supported and well.

Pull up some weeds. Re-pot a plant that's outgrown its home. Sow new seeds. Prune back what's overgrown. Plant or pick fruit and veg.

Each of these tasks is more than simply gardening. They're metaphors in action. What's ready to be let go? What needs more space or care? What's quietly growing just beneath the surface?

Gratitude

Gratitude can ground us on Bad Days and help us find a spark of hope. And while I'm not trying to negate the experience of your Bad Day, focusing on things you are grateful for can be very useful.

Try writing about a time when you felt deeply grateful for something or someone.

Or think back to another challenging event in your life and compare it to how you feel today. Most likely, you will find something to be grateful for, even if it is simply that you got through it and are here now.

Don't ignore that you're feeling bad right now, but try to find that little place deep down that knows you will get through this because you have before. And that is something to be grateful for.

Doing the work

Sometimes a Bad Day needs more than a walk or a journal entry. It needs structure.

One helpful model is Byron Katie's 'The Work',[14] a meditative process of self-inquiry that gently challenges your thoughts and beliefs. Through a few simple questions, you can begin to identify and unravel limiting stories that keep you stuck.

There are many more frameworks that you might find useful available on the internet, providing free tools, exercises and videos.

Take your time, follow your curiosity and see what resonates. It might help you understand not just this Bad Day, but what it's trying to tell you.

Pause point

Every day has a few moments that land a little harder than the rest. It could be a comment, a feeling, a flicker of tension. Instead of letting it rush past, choose one moment and pause with it.

Sit with it for a breath or two. What happened there? What did it touch in you?

You don't have to unpack your whole day – just this one point. A tiny moment of noticing can reveal more than a full hour of overthinking.

Perhaps you could also reflect on what sparked a sense of joy amidst your Bad Day.

Feel your feels

Releasing pent-up emotions, tension and stress can be cathartic. So, sit down, take a breath and admit how you are feeling. Call it out for what it is. Be precise about the words you use. 'You've got to name it to tame it', to use a quote made popular by Dr Phil.[15]

Have a good cry, laugh hysterically, scream, make weird sounds, shout – just feel it and let it come out however it needs to.

Then, when you are ready, stop. Allow your breath to return to normal. Rest deeply.

Wash it away

Soaking in a tub can provide relaxation, stress relief and a sense of comfort, helping to alleviate tension during difficult times. So why not take a nice, long bath to relax and unwind?

Set your bathroom to 'luxuriate'. Light some candles. Sprinkle some rose petals. Choose your playlist. Soak away your cares in mineral salt, bubbles, or my fave – milk, honey and lavender bath oil.

Allow the scents, warmth, sensation of the water and music to create a relaxing ambience. Calmly ponder where you are and the possibilities of what's next.

Online lifeline

Get a handle on your Bad Day by learning about what you are experiencing. There are some great free resources online to help you get through your Bad Day.

If you find you have specific questions about your current mental health, check out the Lifeline Support toolkit. Their quiz asks what's on your mind and what sort of help you are looking for. It collates resources for you – articles, apps and courses that might be helpful. The insights you find may be enough to get you through.

And if you need to reach out, help is a click or a phone call away.

Lifeline:
Call 13 11 14
Text 0477 13 11 14
Toolkit https://toolkit.lifeline.org.au

A few of my favourite things

Make note of other activities you like to do to alleviate a Bad Day, when you want to pause and reflect by yourself.

Talk

You don't think Going It Alone is an option, but you don't want to ignore what's happening. Good for you. Simply deciding that is an important step. Having someone to share your Bad Day concerns with can be very beneficial.

There is nothing like an external perspective on your internal musings to move things along in a positive way. Remember, you need the right other person, maybe even a professional.

 **Upside**

Expressing what's happening, feeling heard, and getting support and advice from a smart, compassionate friend (or health professional) can help you get unstuck. Have you ever had that experience where you heard what you were saying out loud to another person and ... lightbulb? Sometimes, that's all it takes.

Other times, you need an outside perspective. Maybe your Bad Day companion has seen this happen with you before and can identify a pattern you may not be aware of. Maybe they have been in a similar situation. Maybe they can ask just the right questions to move you towards another option or a better outcome.

The great thing is that not only do *you* get something out of it, but helping has benefits for the other person as well. And it builds a stronger connection between you both if you stay open to their advice but don't become a slave to it.

 **Downside**

There are two main things to think about as potential downsides to this approach. The first one is about you and the second one is about them.

So, about you. If you constantly ask for help with small things from the same person, it can become a bit burdensome for them. If the moment you have a slightly Bad Day you call them, it's probably not healthy.

Now, some of you, dear readers, will be immediately worried about this and start labelling yourself as needy and dependent, and concerned for the one friend you share with most often. That concern probably means it's not a big deal for you, and it's just you feeling insecure.

Good friends want to know what's going on for you, and they want to be there and help. However, over-reliance can threaten your friendship, especially when you are not taking responsibility and avoiding meaningful action.

And about them. Who are you asking for help? Are they qualified? Will they give you good counsel? Are you just looking to vent and could just as easily tell this to a stuffed toy? Will they simply agree with everything you say, or will they kindly but firmly challenge you? Are they likely to escalate the drama and assist you in digging deeper into the Bad-ness? Or are they able to help you find a way through?

Now it's time to peruse the menu and taste the many activities that can help you *go in together*. Good luck!

Call me

Connecting with a trusted friend provides emotional support and fresh perspectives on a Bad Day.

Contact a friend to share thoughts, reflections and ideas. In my ideal world, this would be in a nice cafe over a cup of coffee, but you can go wherever you feel comfortable. The physical presence of another person can be comforting and connection is what you are looking for.

But even just texting someone to acknowledge what you are experiencing or calling someone because face-to-face isn't possible can be enough.

Choose the person wisely!

Picnic in the park

Nature, food and conversation create a relaxed and open atmosphere for reflection. So why not take a leisurely stroll with a friend in the park? Find a quiet bench or a spot on the grass to sit, discuss life, share a picnic, and gain some insights.

You are really hitting a quadrella here by incorporating some gentle exercise, good conversation, sharing food and being in nature.

It doesn't have to be anything fancy. It doesn't need to take a really long time. You can catch up with someone during their lunchbreak at a nearby park if they are not too rushed. But take your time if you can.

Exhibition ramble

If galleries are your thing, attend an art exhibition or museum with a friend and discuss the symbolism and emotions behind the artwork.

Sharing reflections on what you observe can take the pressure off discussing the issue. It gives your Bad Day a little time and space and allows it to come out at its own pace, often fed by the exhibits. Enjoy the act of meandering around a public space and engaging with a good friend.

It's a very gentle way to approach and share your concerns.

Body language

Talking is more than words and engaging your mind.

Making time for a professional to 'talk' to your body could be just what you need. Book a session with a massage therapist, Reiki practitioner, acupuncturist, chiropractor, or any other body or energy therapist that suits you.

Spend an hour with someone who can help you listen to your body and interpret what it is saying. In addition to making you more relaxed, body therapy releases some of the tension and energy stuck in your body and can make the path ahead seem clearer.

Remembering yourself

Seeing yourself through the eyes of those who love you can soften the grip of a Bad Day and remind you that you're more than the one struggle that's in front of you right now.

Spend some time reminiscing with someone you've known for a while. Contact an old school friend or an older relative, such as a caring grandparent. Share stories and reflect on your experiences. Look through some old family albums or photos from a trip you took together, or peruse your high school yearbook. It can be nice to recall times that weren't Bad Days.

I recently reconnected with an old friend from high school, and she remembers the parts of me I had long forgotten. It's good to be put back together again.

Pin drop

Step outside of yourself and engage in the shared experience of exploring new environs with someone.

Drop a pin in your map app or flick open to a page in an actual city map and randomly stick a pin in. Go together and find out what is happening there.

It's an opportunity to step away from your usual hangouts and experience something new and exciting, or boring, or unusual. Who knows?

Travel there using a different mode of transport, walk down different streets, and observe a place and people you are not as familiar with. These new perspectives can stimulate conversations that cast a new light on your Bad Day issues.

Literary therapy

For those who love reading, head out to a good bookshop with a friend. They are a great place to re-centre and find all manner of help – books, your friend's perspective, and a laugh.

Look for book titles that relate to your Bad Day.

They can produce some very interesting conversations. Perhaps your companion will have a whole different take on the matter and help you see things anew. You may start to feel lighter and brighter. And then there's the possibility of a wonderful chat with refreshments at the bookshop cafe.

It's not the point, but you may even find a book to read later that will have the 'Aha!' moment you've been looking for. Something to clarify things and help keep your Bad Days at bay. All avenues to achieving our outcomes are welcome.

Seek counsel

A good mental health practitioner will help you understand your Bad Days and give you strategies for success.

So don't rule out talking to a psychologist or therapist. Talk therapy is very effective, and these people have the skills to support you as you pass through Bad Day Land.

Do some research, ask friends for a recommendation, and find the best practitioner for you. The resources section at the back of the book includes links to association websites.

There are also other types of therapies that might be helpful for you too, such as art therapy.

Clean up conversations

Have you heard of three-point communication? Instead of just talking face-to-face, both people focus on a shared third point — like a photo, document, or even a view out the window. This creates a neutral space that makes the conversation feel less direct or intimidating.

A more novel approach involves walking around your neighbourhood with a friend, a pair of gloves and a rubbish bag. As you chat about your Bad Day and other topics, collect any litter that is cluttering up your world.

No judgement, no whining, just do it. No, you didn't put the litter there, but doing your bit is community-minded and very satisfying. Plus, it takes the pressure off constant eye contact and gives you something else to focus on, helping the conversation feel more open.

Closet reset

Fancy peeling away what no longer fits or suits you, and getting talking about what does?

You've probably been meaning to do it for a while anyway, so why not invite a friend to help you organise your wardrobe? Get rid of those items that don't fit, are carbon-dated, or are beyond repair.

It's a shared activity that can be a good way to initiate a conversation about how you feel and see yourself. Certainly not one you want to do by yourself right now.

You can give some things to charity and get some wardrobe space back to accommodate the new you.

LEGO® logic

Grab a handful of LEGO bricks (or any building blocks you have, or even Play-Doh) to create with while you gradually share what's happening. Sounds a bit childish? It's just about giving shape to what's on your mind while keeping your hands busy. This lowers stress and accesses a more playful, creative part of your brain, making it easier to express tough feelings and see them from a fresh perspective.

There's no right or wrong way to do this. Work through answering a couple of questions as you build what's wrong, what's needed, or what the solution could look like. Your Bad Day buddy can make their perspective in LEGO.

Be ready to laugh at the masterpieces you have created and if it feels right, destroy them with vigour.

Warning: Avoid accidentally adding to your Bad Day by standing on dropped LEGO with bare feet.

Hand over

Don't want to do it alone, don't want to ignore what's going on, but can't make a decision? Well, here's an idea. Choose a companion who is available to get together with you.

Let them know you are having a Bad Day and that it would be good to spend time with them and perhaps do something. But as you are not thinking straight, you are putting yourself in their hands.

You are giving them the keys and will go along with whatever they think would be good to do.

Remember, you need to give yourself over to the activity, whatever it is, and trust that you will find the perfect opportunity to share what's on your mind.

Walk'n'talk

Pull on your hiking boots, grab some water and hit the trail with a friend.

Meander by a river, stroll among tall trees, breathe in the clean air, and check out the flying and scurrying critters.

Moving your body and spending time with a friend in nature are wonderful ways to help us heal. Walk. Talk. Listen. Question. Think. Breathe.

Action plan

Set up a workshop vibe in the kitchen with paper, sticky notes, textas, whatever you have on hand, and get ready for both of you to discuss aspirations, set goals and create action plans.

Don't just look for your buddy to give suggestions and advice. Choose someone who is good at asking great questions that allow you to think things through for yourself.

Take turns, because then you can listen to the advice you give, which is sometimes exactly what we need to hear for ourselves.

It can be a proactive approach to finding a longer term solution to your Bad Day with someone who knows you and can ask challenging questions. And you can keep in touch to see how you and your friend are progressing on your plans and help hold each other to account.

Tabletop tournament

Playing a two-person game gives you headspace to think beyond your Bad Day, lets you engage in a pleasant activity with a friend, and allows your concerns to bubble up of their own accord.

If it's not backgammon, which is a favourite of mine, choose something that challenges your brain a little, like chess, Jenga or Scrabble.

In-person is best for a Bad Day, but you could do it online. (Now, imagine me putting my hand to my mouth and coughing to disguise the words, 'Not ideal.')

Relax, refocus and find a non-confrontational way to talk over your Bad Day in good company.

A few of my favourite things

Make note of other activities you like to do to alleviate a Bad Day, when you want to connect with others and reflect.

When we give our pain words, we give it shape. And once it has shape, we can work with it.[16]

Lori Gottlieb

Distract

The Distract approach is a game for one player who needs to get out of their head, give their heart a rest, and just do something nice for themselves, by themselves. If this is what you've chosen, that's brill!

Sometimes, you just don't want to, can't possibly, aren't ready to deal. If you are under stress, you won't be doing your best thinking anyway. Maybe you just need a distraction ... a diversion ... until you are ready to move ahead and maybe get into – or beyond – whatever this is about.

 **Upside**

A distraction can give you the breathing space you need. You can keep your tetchy, sad, cranky self to yourself and not infect your nearest and dearest with your current case of Bad Day-ness.

You're in charge of your distraction. You get to choose, organise and indulge in whatever you need to get clear of the debris.

 ## Downside

While this is healthy in moderation, you can't let distraction become your default. You can create some very unhealthy and even dangerous habits if you visit too often and stay too long.

When things get a bit crappy, it can be very enticing to turn to an alternative form of crappy. If you find you are slipping into poor behaviours to compensate for a Bad Day, it's time to move out of distraction and find another option. And if you can't, get some help.

But for now, enjoy whatever distraction you choose. Try a new one every now and then. Enjoy!

Picture perfect

Grab your camera. If you're old-school, load it with film. Otherwise, charge that digital SLR or phone, and explore.

Photography encourages observation, creativity, and a mindful appreciation of the present moment. So experiment in nature, urban and domestic environments. Get up close, up high, down low, or zoom all the way out to capture interesting perspectives, patterns or vistas.

Examine what's attracting you. Get lost in deep observation, respond to creative impulses, and wonder at the beautiful and interesting that exist right in front of you.

Literary retreat

Dive into a captivating book that transports you to a different world. Let the words enfold you in a comforting embrace as you find solace and refuge from turmoil. Immerse yourself in tales of dark adventure, mysteries, other worlds, and welcome in wisdom, hope and love.

While it doesn't matter where you read, it doesn't hurt to make your experience pleasant – a park bench on a fine day, a cosy fire, a hammock or a comfy couch. Lose yourself for a while and return feeling refreshed after making new fictional acquaintances and stepping outside yourself.

Streaming extravaganza

Binge watch your favourite films or telly series. Veg out, enjoying the entertainment solo when you are completely in charge of the remote. This activity – in its purest form – requires very few additional accessories, but a super comfy couch, some snacks and a tub of your favourite ice-cream probably won't go astray.

Whether you are getting stuck into a long-running series or a movie marathon, this is a classic diversionary activity.

Watching TV can be a welcome form of escapism, offering a needed break from reality and providing a source of joy. However, this passive option is not recommended long term.

Beat surrender

Shut the doors, pull down the blinds, dim the lights, and crank up whatever song demands you move. Then let yourself go. Dance hard, dance silly, dance like your lounge room is a 1980s club. No one will ever know.

It's a joyful, full body reset that boosts endorphins, shakes out stress and lifts your mood whether you've got rhythm or not.

I like to cue up the treasured tracks of my misspent youth, the ones that practically insist you surrender to the beat and throw myself around without a shred of dignity.

So, if it's your jam, come on – succumb to the beat. Simply surrender.

Mindful movement

Do your favourite type of movement that focuses on mindfulness, body awareness, and physical wellbeing. This could be something like yoga, Tai Chi, Qi Gong, Aikido, Feldenkrais or the Alexander Technique. Mindful movement improves flexibility, reduces stress, and promotes a sense of balance and wellbeing.

If you are a beginner, test out something new. There are heaps of free sessions on the internet.

Now, find a peaceful setting and melt into a practice that simultaneously engages your body and mind.

Solo sporty

Get the blood pumping and the happy chemicals happening by trying a new solo sport, or just one that you love. High-intensity sports provide a healthy outlet for stress, boost your confidence, and offer a sense of accomplishment.

If you're looking for an adrenaline rush and a personal challenge, you could go rock climbing, kayaking, or simply find a new trail to explore and bike ride or run your way to a lighter mood.

Shop it

Retail therapy can be a great diversion if you are into it. Getting out to an op shop, a market, the mall, or high street can provide endless opportunities for perusing and purchasing.

Check out your favourite retail category and see what's new. Find whatever floats your shopping boat, be it hardware, stationery, music, books, clothes, plants or shoes.

Maybe you want to buy yourself something nice, buy a gift for someone who is important to you, or just go window shopping and experience the vibe.

And while shopping is comforting (for some) and makes you feel good in the moment, don't create a headache for later by turning into a pelican – big bills.

Solo spa day

Treat yourself to a solo spa day at home, or splurge at a spa or salon. Indulge in relaxation through baths, skincare and pampering. There are so many options that it can be hard to choose.

Self-care practices like spa days promote physical and mental wellbeing, creating a rejuvenating experience.

Take the waters at a mineral springs retreat, try a sauna, spa or steam bath. Have a facial, mani-pedi, or get your hair zhuzhed.

Soul food

Getting into the kitchen and whipping up a storm can be quite therapeutic. Cooking can be a meditative and creative practice with some delicious outcomes.

Got an itch to bake a cake, make the perfect sourdough, cook up some jam or chutney masterpiece, or get a head start on dinners for the week (month, year)?

Cooks have their favourite things about creating dishes, both simple and elaborate. The act of preparing ingredients, the smells and the sounds of the kitchen. Mine is getting to lick the spoon (a childhood memory) or eat the crunchy overcooked end piece of any cooking endeavour.

Then there is the delight of seeing others enjoy the final product. It's a rich, sensual and generous experience.

Cold reset

When your mind is spiralling, sometimes the fastest way out is through your body. A quick hit of cold snaps your system out of its loop.

For beginners, try a splash of water or a chilled drink. If the weather permits, step outside and breathe in some fresh air; otherwise, simply hang out in the cold section of the supermarket.

If you want to ramp it up a little, try a cold shower or an ice bath. It's a small shock that interrupts the sense of overwhelm and gives your brain something new to focus on. Think of it as an emotional reboot button: simple, sharp and surprisingly effective.

Hobby heaven

What's that thing you do where time evaporates and you lose yourself? It doesn't matter what it is – working on a car, woodworking, fishing, jewellery making, mosaicking, whittling, metal detecting, stamp collecting, bird watching, or quilting. It's your happy place. So maybe it's time to go there for a while and give yourself a break.

Breathe, create, fall into a different space and time, and get that deep sense of satisfaction.

The good grind

Throw yourself into a task and tick off a few (or a few dozen) things on your list. It might take some focus to get started, so choose what matches your energy – deep work if you're up for it, or simple no-brainer busywork if that's all you can manage.

Whether it's gluing yourself to the chair to finish paperwork or powering through some active jobs like cleaning, once you get going, you'll not only get things done but you'll experience that lift accomplishment brings.

Smackdown

Push out some of that Bad Day juju and pummel a punching bag. Release pent-up energy, stress and aggression in a controlled environment by getting in some solid hooks and roundhouse kicks.

Strike out at a heavy bag rather than something you can hurt physically or emotionally, like yourself or someone else.

The crazy shouting and shiny costumes are optional, but highly recommended.

Feel better playlist

The link between music, emotions and memory in the brain is very strong. So even if you are feeling down, challenge yourself to create a Feel Good playlist on your music streaming platform or in your digital library.

You will soon be moving from one tune to the next, unable to get all the way through one track because, suddenly, you have thought of another one you love even more.

Then you have a handy playlist ready in case another Bad Day takes hold.

Feeling puzzled

Grab your phone, tablet, book, newspaper or magazine and do some pointless puzzles. Spend some time working through the ups and downs of a crossword. Or count on filling the spaces in a Sudoku. Do a word search or jigsaw. Choose your degree of difficulty and let your mind solve some other dilemma.

Online games can be great, but pick ones that stretch your brain a bit – and set a timer or you might look up and realise it's tomorrow.

A few of my favourite things

Make note of other activities you like to do to alleviate a Bad Day, when you want to distract yourself for a while.

_____

_____

_____

_____

_____

_____

_____

_____

_____

_____

_____

_____

Play

The Play approach asks a very valid question, 'If the Day sucks this Bad, why not just party?' Well done! You can't argue with that.

Getting out and getting together with other people can lift the spirits and be a super-effective Bad Day eraser.

 ## Upside

Being with others in a different and stimulating environment can be just the tonic for excessive Bad Day-ness. There are all sorts of great distractions for more than one player, ages 8 to 80.

But before you start to think that this is all about some hedonistic event, remember, it can be an opportunity to put your focus on the needs of others.

 **Downside**

While partying is fun, and we all need to play, are we simply 'amusing ourselves to death', to quote the late American cultural critic, Neil Postman?[17] Does this become an avoidance technique that stops us from being responsible for our own wellbeing? We have read enough celebrity magazines to know that excessive partying is not the answer.

So, choose your adventure, choose some good company and head out, leaving the Bad Day behind for a while.

Are you game?

Call up a bunch of people and ask them to bring their favourite board, card, parlour game or trivia questions. Nothing hi-tech or digital. Strictly analog.

Get one or more groups together, settle in and let the games and the laughs begin.

I'm bringing a bowl of ideas for charades, Hungry Hungry Hippos and some luscious snacks.

Karaoke carnival

Hit the karaoke bar for a night of singing, dancing and infectious laughter with friends.

No venue around? There are machines for hire or some great apps.

Get amongst some colourful lights as everyone sings their hearts out to their favourite tunes. And brace yourself for the surprise of discovering that one of your friends has an incredible voice.

Comedy improv night

Boost your happy hormones and go to a local stand-up comedy or improv show with friends for an evening of spontaneous laughter. Small venues in most cities have people who are just starting out or established performers trying new material.

If you are feeling game, find an open-mic night and give it a red-hot go yourself. Bad Days give you plenty of fodder, so try sharing it with a group of strangers in a dark venue.

If it's fun you might try taking a stand-up or improv course and, who knows, launch a new career.

Not your everyday sports

Kicking, hitting or throwing a ball around is always fun, but why not mix it up? Try a sport that you and your friends haven't done before (or rarely get to play). The novelty makes it even more entertaining, and everyone can join in – whether you're brilliant or hilariously bad.

How about indoor climbing, ice skating, archery, axe throwing, bowling, paintballing, go-karting, ultimate frisbee, indoor skydiving, or pickleball? Together, you can get a bit fitter, make mistakes, and turn the competitive dial down (or up) as you simply have some fun.

Lunch in the park

Invite friends and family to a park party. Bring food, drinks, comfy seating, things to read and games. Spend the afternoon eating, drinking, snoozing, playing games and laughing.

It's easy to organise, relaxing, low-cost and fun. Being surrounded by lots of people you love and who care about you is a great tonic. Do it often.

And when the weather isn't cooperating, get creative. Relax and embrace the vicissitudes of the season under a canopy, on tarps and wearing climate-appropriate attire. Or simply recreate your picnic indoors.

Solve-it session

Channel your inner detective and book an escape room or murder mystery event with a group of your nearest and dearest. Test your thinking with these challenging activities and create some hilarious shared memories.

Work with friends to unravel clues, solve puzzles and uncover the truth before time runs out. Immerse yourself in a heart-pounding adventure where every twist and turn brings you closer to cracking the case. Go on. Release your inner Sherlock.

Go clubbing

Turn up the volume on a night out with a group of besties at your favourite dance emporium. Embrace that primal urge to move to music. Lose yourself to the pulsating beats and luminous lights. Let your hair down as you set the dancefloor on fire, laughing and enjoying a drink or two.

It's not a night for talking or thinking about Bad Days. Just get down and boogie (yes, I am that old). However, it could be wise to consider the cost-benefit analysis of a hangover early in the event.

Get out of town

Take yourself and a group of people you love out of your routine and your geography. Enjoy a road trip. Camp under the stars. Book a shared house. Stay in a luxury hotel. Just get out of town together.

Change your scenery and be a tourist. Explore new things, discovering the region's hidden treasures. Chill and share time together, which can be scarce in our busy lives.

Or do a little of both. Make it easy for people to choose their own adventures and balance that with connecting with the group.

Take in a show

Get a few people together and go see a show. Maybe a play, concert, ballet, opera, comedy show or musical – whatever appeals to you. As it's likely this Bad Day event is an impulse thing, check out what's available at a discount for last-minute tickets and leave it up to chance a little.

Enjoy sitting in the dark theatre and being entertained by dedicated and talented performers who take you on an emotional journey and leave you richer for the experience. Share your excitement, bemusement or confusion with your friends, feeling happy that you went along together.

Take a class

Learn a new skill and meet other people with similar interests and different experiences. A shared struggle can make the process easier and often funnier.

Engage your body and mind as you learn to juggle, make unrecognisable pottery, belly dance, get crafty with textiles, or try cooking.

The choice is endless.

Plus, you now have a new activity you can do on any future Bad Days.

Cinema escape

Gather the gang and head to the cinema. Choose a fun and distracting movie – a rom-com, action, thriller or horror flick. Dive into the whole experience with a bucket of popcorn, sugary drink and Choc Top.

Or, if you are up for a splurge, go for the luxury option that comes with a special food and beverage service. Maybe even arrange your own private showing.

With easy access to streaming services, we are doing this less and less. So, some film therapy in a real cinema can be a nice bit of nostalgia for you and your peeps.

Video games night

Get some of your gamer friends (see what I did there), set up a couple of gaming stations, drinks and nibbles, a championship board, and have a gaming party.

Play each other in a series of games that produces an overall champion with bragging rights until the next event. Don't take it too seriously. Don't get stuck in one never-ending game. Get a healthy dose of competition and have some seriously good fun.

Sail away together

Row down the river, sail on the sea, but get off terra firma with a few friends. You don't need your Yachtmaster or Coxswain certificates. It can be fun to take a ferry ride somewhere, feel the fresh air and enjoy those negative ions. Hire a rowboat and paddle upstream. Drift away on giant tubes. Or sail off into the sunset on a cruise.

Alternatively, float high above the earth in a hot air balloon. Unground yourselves and experience the world differently.

High Tea

Put on your nice duds and go somewhere a bit swish for High Tea. Sip champagne and gaze around the beautiful room. Savour orange pekoe from an exquisite porcelain tea set featuring elegant curves, delicate floral patterns and gilded accents.

Make your way through the tiered cake stand as you enjoy the tiny, tasty savoury and sweet morsels before hitting the scones and getting into arguing about the correct way to apply jam and cream to those warm, cloud-soft hugs.

It's such a yummy – and just a bit special – way to celebrate life and the people you love. No other reason is required.

Cheer squad

Barrack for your team playing your favourite sport. Maybe it's the professional leagues or your friends' kids playing in the park. Get behind them.

Partake in the group ritual of respectfully disagreeing with the ref when their decision goes against your players. Shout yourself hoarse as you encourage better play or appreciate breathtaking spectacles of sports-personship. And all the while holding on to the delusion that you are a critical part of the team and solely responsible for their victories rather than just the cheer squad (LOL).

A few of my favourite things

Make note of other activities you like to do to alleviate a Bad Day by spending time with friends in the fun-est way possible.

What if it doesn't work?

So, you went to do something, but your Bad Day-ness got in the way. Let's check out a couple of ways that can happen.

You couldn't find the quadrant

When you absolutely have no decision-making capabilities, try this. Grab a coin, ask the question and allocate heads or tails to a specific answer. Leave it to the fates. I often do this if I can't decide on something. Then I stay attuned to how I feel when the coin lands. If I am really disappointed, I know it's not what I want and I choose the alternative. But you do you.

You couldn't choose the activity

You've found your quadrant, but you can't pick an activity. Well, you can try randomising this as well.

Go to any section in this book and flip the pages.

The one you stop on is the one you try. Or write down the names of activities that interest you (a good distracting activity in itself), pop them in a hat and then draw one out. Commit to trying whatever comes out.

You made a choice, but you couldn't make the effort

Yeah, you picked something, but you couldn't be bothered trying it. Well, you're still stuck.

Ask yourself the first question again: 'Do you really want to get unstuck and shake off the Bad Day?'

I know it's tough.

Pop back to the 'Staying stuck' section and get into being full-on stuck if you aren't making headway.

You weren't built with today's fast-paced, distracting, turvy-topsy world in mind. All you can do is try the things you believe will help you feel a little better.

What other positive experiment could you try?

It wasn't really what you wanted to do

Tried it.

Didn't like it.

Simple.

Try something else.

You couldn't find someone to do it with

This can be trickier. Getting together with people who inconveniently have their own lives to live can be difficult on short notice. Here are a few things to try.

- Focus on planning for the get-together.
- Maybe there is someone else you haven't immediately thought of who could help.
- Try a short distraction activity until you can meet.

And always remember, if you need more serious help immediately, call a helpline.

You couldn't focus

You gave your thing a red-hot go but found it difficult to focus on the activity. Your mind kept cycling through Bad Day stuff. That can happen, so don't get too down on yourself.

Like meditation, make a choice each time a distracting thought comes to mind. You can stop and focus on the thought or take a deep breath and return to what you were doing.

If you were Going Out, your thoughts may signal that it's time to come in for a while. Just try to be conscious and deliberate about the choices you make.

At times, I have to engage with the voice in my head that's telling me the many ways I am wrong. I call her Aunt Doris. I know she is trying to keep me safe in her own (deluded) way. So, I tell her, 'Thanks, Doris, but I am doing this,' while pointing straight ahead, signifying I am choosing to move forward.

You had other obligations

The thing you wanted to do wasn't possible. You had kids, work or other responsibilities. You could try acknowledging what you want to do and commit to making it happen as soon as you can.

But if Bad Days are a now thing for you, what can you do?

Find something simple to do, even if it's sitting on a park bench, putting your bare feet on the grass and taking a moment to breathe.

This too shall pass

Whatever happened with your Bad Day remedy, remember, you will come through this. It's a Bad Day – or afternoon, or hour, or minute. It will pass.

In the meantime, why not try something else? Make it something completely different from the last thing.

Keep in mind that at the very least, you have managed to distract yourself by contemplating your Bad Day options for a while.

Now go back to the start and ask the questions. Or have a nap or a snack. Doing something to move through this is better than nothing.

But now, let's briefly delve into another approach altogether.

Embrace the glorious mess that you are.[18]

Elizabeth Gilbert

Obviously, you would really prefer not to have Bad Days to begin with. For most of us they aren't always avoidable, but we now have access to a plan for taking action and moving through them. Thanks, *Bad Day Playbook* suggestions.

Now that you are through the immediate relief phase, it might be useful to consider a couple of ways to be a little more proactive, rather than just reacting to Bad Days as they occur. So, how do we make them less frequent, decrease their power over us, see them coming, or see them differently?

When you know that bad things aren't so terrible and good things aren't so terrific, you can be quietly grateful for whatever occurs.[19]

John F Demartini

Good, bad or something else

An old fable tells of a farmer who was proud of his mare and depended on her for his labour. Day after day, they ploughed the fields, and this hard work brought him a steady income. Then, one day, the horse escaped. The farmer's neighbours lamented his bad luck, but he simply said, 'Good luck, bad luck, who knows?'

Then, a day or so later, the mare returned, bringing with her two more horses, and making the neighbours envious of the farmer's newfound fortune. They praised his good luck, but the farmer remained indifferent, saying, 'Good luck, bad luck, who knows?'

A little while later, the farmer's son broke his leg while working with the new horses. Now the neighbours decried his bad luck, as the farmer's son couldn't help with the planting. Again, the farmer shrugged, saying, 'Good luck, bad luck, who knows?'

A week later, the Emperor set about conscripting the young men in the surrounding areas to fight in the war, but the son was spared due to his injury, leaving the neighbours to acknowledge the family's good luck.

The farmer's response remained constant throughout each event: 'Good luck, bad luck, who knows?'

It's a bit like that with Bad Days. You can't avoid crappy things happening. Sometimes, you just have to get through the day the best you can. But as this fable demonstrates, we can't always know what will come out of some action or incident. This bit of so-called 'Bad' could give us an insight or move us somewhere we didn't expect to be. Our challenges can make us stronger or teach us important things. And an incredible windfall may not be as wonderful as we first imagined.

Who knows?

But sometimes things happen that aren't so good. When they occur, I've learned that there's not much you can do except stand tall and reach deep.[20]

Katherine Applegate

Being a bit stoic

What if we stopped thinking of the Bad Day as Bad? It's just a day. As Shakespeare wrote, 'There is nothing either good or bad, but thinking makes it so.'[21]

The Stoics, followers of a school of philosophy that flourished in Ancient Greece and Rome, contended that there are things in life you can control and things you can't. They believed you should remain indifferent to the things outside your control, much like the farmer in our tale – things such as death, illness, wealth, status, etc. And while we prefer to be alive, healthy, wealthy, and have good status, we can't always rely on life turning out that way.

However, some things are in our control, and we should focus on cultivating them. Stoics identified these as our character, our actions and reactions, and how we treat others. We should not waste our time or energy worrying about things beyond our control.

We can control our emotions, reactions to outside events, and the actions we take each day. Our boss being an arse, getting dumped, losing your phone, or becoming ill are not in our control. Some things simply happen. So, remember the popular song by the cartoon princess with that strange ice impediment and 'Let it go'.[22]

You can't choose what happens, but you can choose how you react and what you do next. Doing something to get through and beyond your Bad Day shows a positive aspect of your character. Just as taking your Bad Day out on others or yourself says the opposite.

Working through your Bad Days can shift to proactively avoiding them (mostly) by making sure you regularly incorporate the ideas offered in the Playbook (and the others that you add to it yourself) in everyday life. Do a little more of the things that nourish you and bring you joy consistently.

A proactive playbook

Now, I am going to let you in on a little secret.

It was a Bad Day that led me to stumble on an idea to help myself work through them. At first, haphazardly and then diligently, I started curating a list on my phone of things I could do to get me through my Bad Day. I created a little model to make identification easier. Then I started writing these ideas into a book-like format. And it turned out that I was inventing something that was already invented – well, at least partially.

D'oh!

I wondered if there is a word for that because it's happened to me more than once. Turns out, there is. Urban Dictionary tells me that *revent* is one. They define it as: 'When a person independently invents something new, while being oblivious to the fact that it has already been invented by someone else.'[23]

It's also referred to more colloquially as 'Pulled a Leibniz', named after the mathematician Gottfried Wilhelm Leibniz, who 'thought his fancy maths were something new, but in reality, they had already been found eight years earlier by Isaac Newton'.[24]

Another suggestion on the web for this phenomenon is that it's due to insufficiently rigorous research. Ouch! That hurts.

Anyhow, it turns out I have *revented* Behavioural Activation (BA). It's used as part of Cognitive Behavioural Therapy (CBT) or can be a standalone therapy, and it is at least as effective as antidepressant medication (which you should never cease taking without the support of your medical practitioner).

Here is a description:

> BA is a way of changing from the outside in – jump-starting individuals back to the kind of life they once enjoyed. Evidence suggests that even in small doses, engaging in a constructive activity is positively reinforcing, not only rekindling interest in and energy for the activity but providing a sense of achievement – enough to disrupt the negative feelings, avoidant behavior, and disturbed mood that keep people trapped in depression, and the avoidant behavior that is the hallmark of anxiety.[25]

Now, what I am suggesting here is that you don't wait for a Bad Day. Make sure you are finding time to get out and about by yourself and with others. Make sure you are finding time to sit and reflect on things that need to be pondered. Do it deeply and with curiosity and compassion, because these ponderable things are important and awesome. And talk with a friend about what's going on – someone you trust to be kind and honest. This will help eliminate or lessen the stuck-ness in your life and bring you more joy and fulfilment.

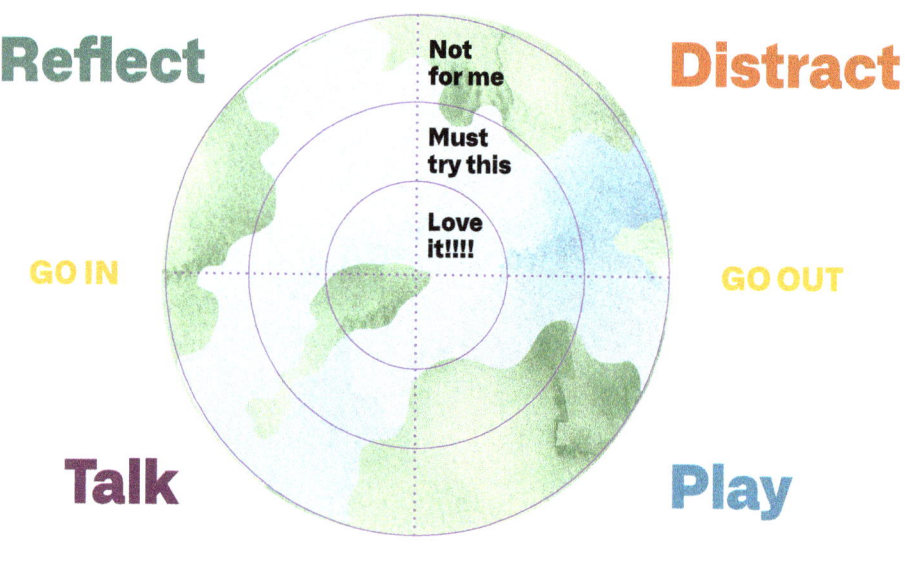

Map out a plan for some of the things you want to try, some things you love to do and stuff that's not for you. Find ways to build in some basic actions and activities that help, and make them a habit. A regular catch-up with a friend. Swimming twice a week. A 10-minute neck massage at the shopping centre before you do the grocery shopping. And aim to do a couple of new things over the next few months.

Don't fall into the trap of trying to do a whole bunch of things because you are excited by the ideas in this book and by generally taking ownership of feeling better (maybe mostly that last one). Take small, consistent actions. Build over time. It's not as sexy as the big transformational plan, but it's more sustainable.

While I don't wish anyone Bad Days, they can give us space to think, rest and develop ways to be more resilient and forgiving of ourselves and others. I hope this book helps you to get a handle on how to manage life when everything sucks. And offers you some ways to limit the impact and intensity of Bad Days, so you can work towards making them either a thing of the past or nothing you can't handle.

Contacts

Helplines

13YARN – 13 92 76 (24/7 support for Aboriginal and Torres Strait Islander people)

Beyond Blue – 1300 22 4636 (24/7 support for anxiety, depression, mental health)

Kids Helpline – 1800 55 1800 (24/7 free, confidential support for ages 5–25)

Lifeline – 13 11 14 (24/7 crisis support and suicide prevention)

MensLine Australia – 1300 789 978 (24/7 support for men, mental health and relationships)

Suicide Call Back Service – 1300 659 467 (24/7 professional counselling for people at risk)

Find a therapist in Australia

Referrals

Ask your GP or primary care doctor for a referral – many therapists require or welcome this pathway.

Professional networks, such as teachers, clergy, or HR/employee assistance programs often keep lists of trusted therapists.

Talk to friends, family or colleagues you trust, if you feel comfortable. Personal recommendations can help you narrow down the search.

Check out reliable, searchable directories

Australian Counselling Association (ACA) can help you find a counsellor. Australia's largest professional body for counsellors and psychotherapists.

Australian Psychological Society (APS) can help you find a psychologist. The main national body for psychologists, searchable by location, specialty, language, etc.

Apps

MindSpot is a free, confidential, online mental health clinic developed in Australia. It provides:

- Screening assessments.
- Internet-delivered Cognitive Behavioural Therapy (iCBT) courses for issues like anxiety and depression.

Smiling Mind is a Melbourne-based non-profit mindfulness and meditation app, completely free. It offers more than 700 audio programs for meditation and mental wellness, suitable for all ages.

Talked is an Australian app designed to connect you with qualified psychologists and counsellors across the country. Features include:

- Medicare and private health rebates, no subscription or joining fees.
- Matching tools to connect you based on your needs.
- No wait times – you can speak to someone within hours.
- Offers messaging, phone, and video sessions, with a free 15-minute video consultation to test the fit.

Yooli is another Australian option offering video sessions with qualified therapists. It lets you:

- Browse therapist profiles by specialisation.
- Schedule therapy during evenings and weekends.

Internationally recognised therapy and mental health apps

BetterHelp and **Talkspace** are two of the most frequently recommended online therapy platforms featuring licensed professionals. They include:

- Access through video, chat, voice or messaging.
- BetterHelp often offers financial aid.
- Talkspace may provide psychiatric services.

These are some options that might help. They may be good places to start when things feel tough. Use what works for you and, remember, you don't have to do it alone.

The information in these pages was accurate at the time I wrote this book. However, things change and some of these resources may no longer be available. If you can't find what you need here, talk to someone who can point you in the right direction, or contact a trusted health professional, your GP or a reputable national helpline.

Bad Day resources

If you found this book helpful, there's more waiting for you.

Head to my website for free templates, new plays as they're released, and the occasional bit of merch designed to support you on the days when everything feels a bit ... much.

You can order a copy of the book to give to a friend, sign up for updates, and see what else I'm cooking up to help you make Bad Days a little less terrible.

Visit: gaylesmerdon.com

Until then,

Gayle Smerdon

Endnotes

1. B Obama, *The best way to not feel hopeless is to get up and do something ...*, AZQuotes, (n.d.). Retrieved 24 August 2025 from AZQuotes.com
2. *I'm just going to put an 'Out of order' sticker on my forehead and call it a day*: Blank lined journal, Amazon.com, 2019. www.amazon.com/dp/1694513963
3. Author's conversation with Functional Medicine Practitioner & Naturopath, Susan Hunter, www.susanhunter.com.au
4. *Was it a bad day or was it a bad 5 minutes that you milked all day?* Inspired to Reality, 9 May 2016. www.inspiredtoreality.com/pin/was-it-a-bad-day-or-was-it-a-bad-5-minutes-that-you-milked-all-day/
5. D Nield, 'Sleep deprivation has the same effect as drinking too much, says study', *ScienceAlert*, 7 November 2017. www.sciencealert.com/tiredness-sleep-deprivation-the-same-as-drinking-too-much
6. P Cook, Workshop presented at Thought Leaders Immersion, Melbourne, Australia, March 2020.
7. C Chaplin, *Nothing is permanent in this world, not even our troubles* [Quote], (n.d.). Retrieved 24 August 2025, from www.goodreads.com/quotes/11007-nothing-is-permanent-in-this-world-not-even-our-troubles

8   A Basich, *You can't get to the top by sitting on your bottom* [Pinterest post], Pinterest, (n.d.). Retrieved 24 August 2025, from https://au.pinterest.com/pin/you-cant-get-to-the-top-by-sitting-on-your-bottom--289356344833188207/
9   'If every day of life is a gift all I keep getting is socks' posted by user Runs With Hatchet (@theanghellicone), 4 August 2009. Reposted by Wade Wilson (@wade_wilson) as 'To quote a great internet sage: if everyday is a gift, then today was socks', 13 August 2010.
10 NASA Space Place, *What is a black hole?*, NASA, 29 August 2022. Retrieved 24 August 2025, from https://spaceplace.nasa.gov/black-holes/en/
11 Commonly attributed to Winston Churchill (origin unverified), International Churchill Society, 10 April 2012. *If you're going through hell, keep going* [Quote investigation]. International Churchill Society. https://winstonchurchill.org/resources/quotes/if-youre-going-through-hell-keep-going/
12 HA Hsu, 'The unexpected benefits of classical music', *Psychology Today*, October 2024. Retrieved 24 August 2025, from www.psychologytoday.com/us/blog/the-flow-of-creativity/202410/the-unexpected-benefits-of-classical-music
13 A Sharma, V Madaan & FD Petty, 'Exercise for Mental Health', *Primary Care Companion* to *The Journal of Clinical Psychiatry*, 8(2), p. 106, 2006. https://doi.org/10.4088/pcc.v08n0208a
14 B Katie, *The work*, Byron Katie International, (n.d.). Retrieved 24 August 2025, from https://thework.com/instruction-the-work-byron-katie/

15 Originally from DJ Siegel & TP Bryson, *The whole-brain child: 12 revolutionary strategies to nurture your child's developing mind*. Delacorte Press, 2011.
16 L Gottlieb, *Maybe you should talk to someone*, Houghton Mifflin Harcourt, 2019.
17 N Postman, *Amusing ourselves to death: Public discourse in the age of show business*, Viking Penguin, 1985.
18 E Gilbert, *Big Magic*, Riverhead Books, 2015.
19 John F Demartini, *The Breakthrough Experience: A Revolutionary New Approach to Personal Transformation*, Hay House, Inc., 2002.
20 Katherine Applegate, *Wishtree*, Feiwel & Friends, 2017.
21 W Shakespeare, *Hamlet,* in S Wells & G Taylor (Eds), *The Oxford Shakespeare: The complete works*, Oxford University Press, 1992, pp 653–706. (Original work published 1603.)
22 K Anderson-Lopez & R Lopez, *'Let it go'* [Song recorded by IMenzel]. On *Frozen: Original motion picture soundtrack*, Walt Disney Records. 2013.
23 Urban Duolingo, *Revent* [Entry on Urban Dictionary], *Urban Dictionary*, 6 October 2022. Retrieved 24 August 2025, from www.urbandictionary.com/define.php?term=Revent
24 Fenhl, *Pulled a Leibniz* [Entry on Urban Dictionary], 23 December 2013, *Urban Dictionary*. Retrieved 24 August 2025, from www.urbandictionary.com/define.php?term=Pulled%20a%20Leibniz
25 Psychology Today Staff, 'Behavioral activation', *Psychology Today*, 3 June 2023. Retrieved 24 August 2025, from www.psychologytoday.com/au/therapy-types/behavioral-activation

First published in Australia in 2026 by Dr Gayle Smerdon
hello@gaylesmerdon.com

Copyright © Dr Gayle Smerdon, 2026
The moral rights of the author have been asserted.

A catalogue record for this work is available from
the National Library of Australia

ISBN: 978-1-7638250-8-6 (Paperback)

All rights reserved. Except as permitted under the *Australian Copyright Act 1968* (for example, fair dealing for the purposes of study, research, criticism or review) no part of this book may be reproduced, stored in a retrieval system, communicated or transmitted in any form or by any means without prior written permission from the author. All enquiries should be made to the author: hello@gaylesmerdon.com

Produced by Broadcast Books, www.broadcastbooks.com.au
Cover and text design and typesetting by Matthew Oswald, Like Design, likedesign.com.au
Cover illustration designed by coolvector / Freepik
Author photograph by Jacinta Cubis
Printed by IngramSpark

Broadcast Books acknowledges Aboriginal and Torres Strait Islander peoples as the first storytellers of this nation and the Traditional Custodians of the land on which we live and work. We acknowledge their continuing culture and pay respects to Elders past and present.

www.ingramcontent.com/pod-product-compliance
Lightning Source LLC
Chambersburg PA
CBHW061119070526
44583CB00028B/3335